INSIDE YOUR BODY

ALL ABOUT ALLERGIES

FRANCESCA POTTS, RN

Consulting Editor, Diane Craig, MA/Reading Specialist

Super Sandcastle

An Imprint of Abdo Publishing
abdopublishing.com

ABDOPUBLISHING.COM

Published by Abdo Publishing, a division of ABDO, PO Box 398166, Minneapolis, Minnesota 55439. Copyright © 2018 by Abdo Consulting Group, Inc. International copyrights reserved in all countries. No part of this book may be reproduced in any form without written permission from the publisher. Super SandCastle™ is a trademark and logo of Abdo Publishing.

Printed in the United States of America,
North Mankato, Minnesota
062017
092017

Production: Mighty Media, Inc.
Editor: Megan Borgert-Spaniol
Cover Photographs: iStock, Shutterstock
Interior Photographs: iStock, Shutterstock

Publisher's Cataloging-in-Publication Data
Names: Potts, Francesca, author.
Title: All about allergies / by Francesca Potts, RN.
Description: Minneapolis, MN : Abdo Publishing, 2018. I Series:
    Inside your body
Identifiers: LCCN 2016962886 I ISBN 9781532111150 (lib. bdg.) I
    ISBN 9781680789003 (ebook)
Subjects: LCSH: Allergy--Juvenile literature.
Classification: DDC 616.97--dc23
LC record available at http://lccn.loc.gov/2016962886

Super SandCastle™ books are created by a team of professional educators, reading specialists, and content developers around five essential components—phonemic awareness, phonics, vocabulary, text comprehension, and fluency—to assist young readers as they develop reading skills and strategies and increase their general knowledge. All books are written, reviewed, and leveled for guided reading, early reading intervention, and Accelerated Reader™ programs for use in shared, guided, and independent reading and writing activities to support a balanced approach to literacy instruction.

CONTENTS

YOUR BODY

You're amazing! So is your body.

Most of the time your body works just fine. It lets you go to school, play with friends, and more. But sometimes you feel sick or part of you hurts.

Allergies can make you uncomfortable or sick. Millions of kids have them. But they find ways to treat their allergies. Then they feel better!

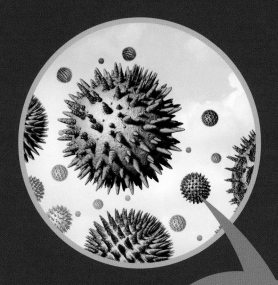

ALLERGEN
(AL-ur-jen)

something that causes an allergic reaction

DO YOU HAVE ALLERGIES?

ALL ABOUT ALLERGIES

H ave you ever had an allergic reaction? This is your body's response to an allergen. It thinks the allergen is harmful. It releases histamines. These help get rid of the allergen.

Common Allergens

AIR: dust mites, pollen, molds, fur

FOOD: dairy, eggs, peanuts, wheat

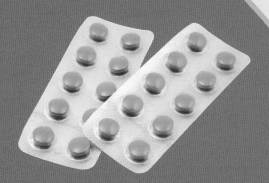

MEDICINE: antibiotics

CHEMICALS: makeup, household cleaners, dyes

INSECT VENOM: bee stings

HISTAMINES
(*HISS-tah-meens*)
······································
chemicals in the body that react to allergens

ALLERGY
TESTING

A doctor can test you for allergies. This will show which allergens affect you. It can also help prevent very bad allergic reactions. Doctors do skin tests and blood tests.

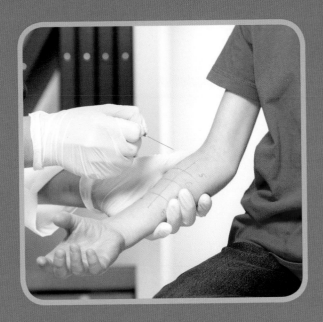

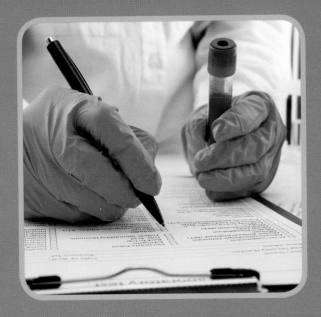

Skin Tests

The doctor uses a needle. She places a small amount of the allergen beneath the skin. **Hives** will appear if there is an allergy.

Blood Tests

The doctor draws some blood. Then she exposes it to different allergens. The level of **antibodies** in the blood is measured. This shows if there is an allergy.

SIGNS
AND SYMPTOMS

Allergic reactions are often mild. But they can sometimes be serious. Here are some common reactions.

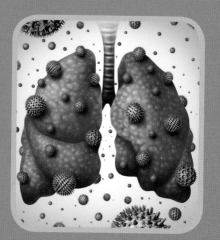

Air allergens

SNEEZING

STUFFY OR RUNNY NOSE

ITCHY, WATERY, RED EYES

COUGHING

SCRATCHY THROAT

Food, medicine, and insect venom allergens

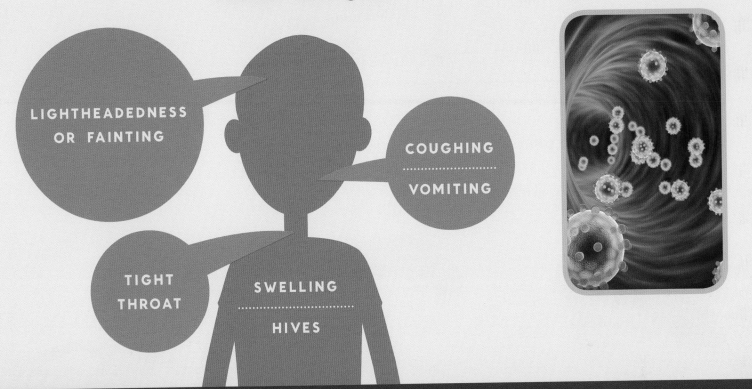

LIGHTHEADEDNESS OR FAINTING

COUGHING

VOMITING

TIGHT THROAT

SWELLING

HIVES

Warning!

Allergies can change over time. You may have had mild **symptoms** in the past. But they could be worse next time. Avoid the allergen whenever possible!

CAUSES

Why do some people have allergies and not others? Doctors are not sure. But they do know that certain people are more likely to have allergies.

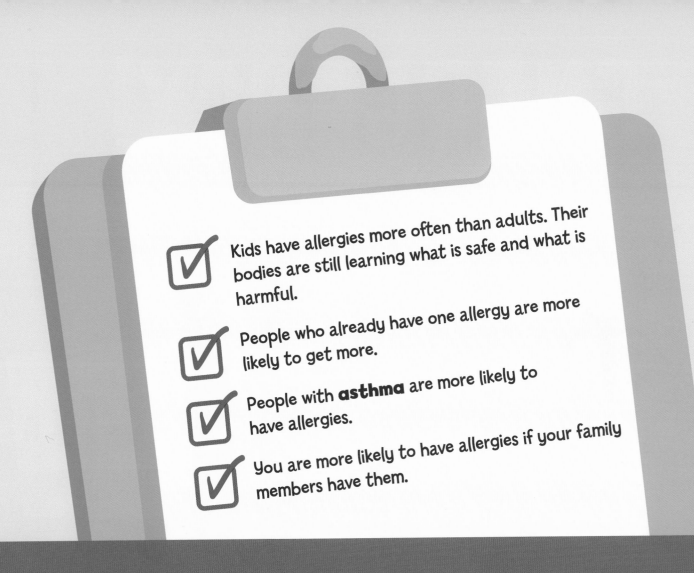

- ☑ Kids have allergies more often than adults. Their bodies are still learning what is safe and what is harmful.

- ☑ People who already have one allergy are more likely to get more.

- ☑ People with **asthma** are more likely to have allergies.

- ☑ You are more likely to have allergies if your family members have them.

Don't Worry

You cannot pass allergies to your friends!

EMERGENCY!

Sometimes an allergic reaction is very serious. This is usually caused by food, medicine, or insect **venom** allergies. **Symptoms** can take hold in seconds. They get worse fast. Call 9-1-1 or go to an **emergency** room right away!

ANAPHYLAXIS
(*anna-fil-LAX-iss*)

a very serious allergic reaction

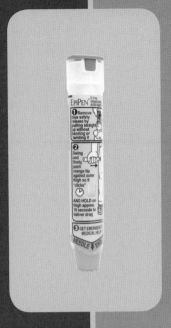

EpiPen

The best medicine for a serious allergic reaction is epinephrine. An EpiPen is a shot of this medicine. You can keep the shot with you all the time. Always go to the **emergency** room right after using an EpiPen.

Symptoms

- Nausea and vomiting

- Difficulty breathing

- Throat closing

- **Hives**

- Fast heartbeat

- Dizziness

- Fainting

ASTHMA
AND ECZEMA

Asthma is a condition that affects your breathing. Allergens can **trigger** an asthma attack. The pathway from the nose and mouth to the lungs becomes swollen. This makes it hard to breathe.

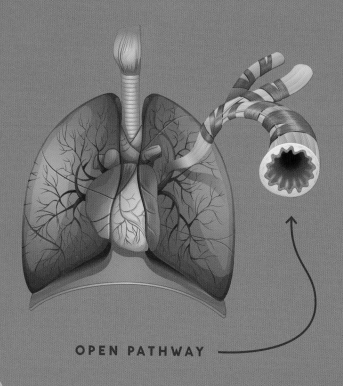

OPEN PATHWAY

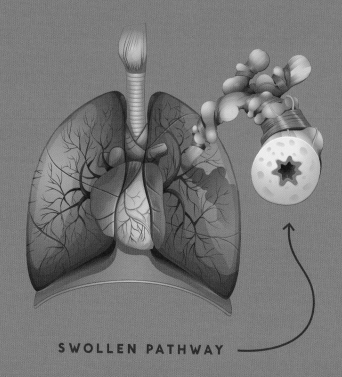

SWOLLEN PATHWAY

Eczema is another condition. It makes the skin break out in a dry, itchy **rash**. Allergens can **trigger** an eczema outbreak.

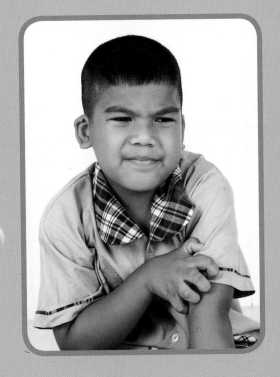

COMMON ASTHMA AND ECZEMA ALLERGENS

FUR

MILK

WHEAT

NUTS

POLLEN

TREATMENT

There is no cure for allergies. But you can still manage or prevent **symptoms**.

- Avoid the allergen.

- Take allergy medicine to lessen **symptoms**.

- Ask your doctor about allergy shots.

- Keep an EpiPen on hand if you have ever had a serious allergic reaction.

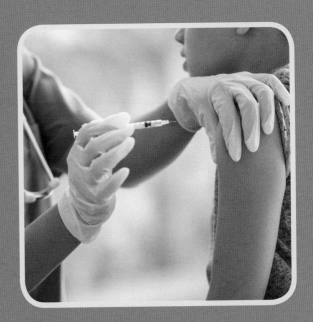

Do you think you have allergies? Talk to your doctor about the best way to treat them.

Allergy Shots

Sometimes regular allergy medicine is not enough. Allergy shots give a small dose of an allergen. This helps your body get used to it. Symptoms lessen over time.

MEDICINES

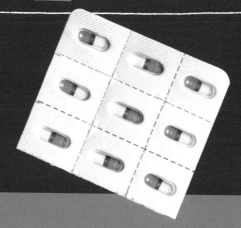

Medicines can treat allergies. They can also save your life in the case of a bad reaction.

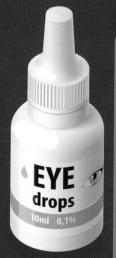

- Remember histamines? They cause your allergy **symptoms**. Antihistamines are medicines. They stop the effects of histamines.

- Eye drops treat dry, itchy eyes.

- **Nasal** sprays treat stuffy and runny noses.

- Epinephrine treats symptoms of anaphylaxis.

NATURAL
REMEDIES

Y ou can also try some natural remedies at home.

- Green tea is a natural antihistamine.

- Hot and spicy foods help clear your nose.

- A **nasal** rinse flushes allergens from the nose.

PREVENTION

You cannot control what you are allergic to. But you can do your best to stop allergic reactions from happening.

LEARN ABOUT THE ALLERGENS THAT AFFECT YOU.

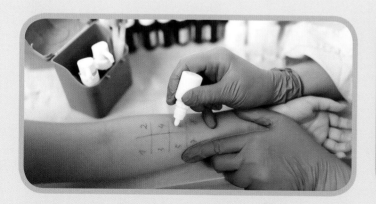

ASK YOUR DOCTOR ABOUT ALLERGY TESTING.

CLEAN AND DUST OFTEN.

AVOID ANIMALS THAT CAUSE REACTIONS.

WEAR AN EMERGENCY ALERT BRACELET. THIS SHOWS WHAT ALLERGIES YOU HAVE.

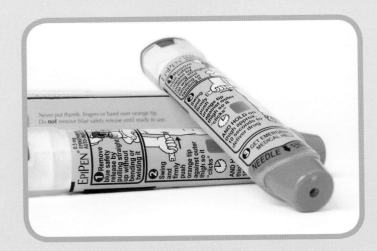

CARRY AN EPIPEN. SEEK MEDICAL HELP IF YOU MUST USE IT.

The number one way to prevent a reaction is to avoid your allergens!

ANTIBIOTIC - a substance used to kill germs that cause disease.

ANTIBODY - something produced by cells in the body to fight off allergens or other unfamiliar matter.

EMERGENCY - a sudden, unexpected, dangerous situation that requires immediate attention.

HIVES - red, itchy, raised patches of skin.

NASAL - relating to the nose.

RASH - a breaking out of spots on the skin.

SYMPTOM - a noticeable change in the normal working of the body.

TRIGGER - to cause something to happen.

VENOM - a poison made by some animals and insects. It usually enters a victim through a bite or a sting.

GLOSSARY